ALLEN SMITH

Memorizing 1 Corinthians 14 - Prophecy, Tongues, and Orderly Worship

Memorize Scripture, Memorize the Bible, and Seal God's Word in Your Heart

First published by Nelaco Press 2021

Copyright © 2021 by Allen Smith

All rights reserved. No part of this publication may be reproduced, stored or transmitted in any form or by any means, electronic, mechanical, photocopying, recording, scanning, or otherwise without written permission from the publisher. It is illegal to copy this book, post it to a website, or distribute it by any other means without permission.

Scripture quotations are from The ESV® Bible (The Holy Bible, English Standard Version®), copyright © 2001 by Crossway, a publishing ministry of Good News Publishers. Used by permission. All rights reserved.

First edition

ISBN: 978-1-952381-56-0

This book was professionally typeset on Reedsy.
Find out more at reedsy.com

To my Lord and Savior

Contents

Before You Begin	1
Introduction	2
How To Use This Book	4
Week 1 Prep Work	6
1 Corinthians 14:1	9
1 Corinthians 14:2	11
1 Corinthians 14:3	13
1 Corinthians 14:4	15
1 Corinthians 14:5	17
1 Corinthians 14:6	19
Week 2 Prep Work	22
1 Corinthians 14:7	24
1 Corinthians 14:8	26
1 Corinthians 14:9	28
1 Corinthians 14:10	30
1 Corinthians 14:11	32
1 Corinthians 14:12	34
Week 3 Prep Work	36
1 Corinthians 14:13	38
1 Corinthians 14:14	40
1 Corinthians 14:15	42
1 Corinthians 14:16	44
1 Corinthians 14:17	46
1 Corinthians 14:18	48
Week 4 Prep Work	50
1 Corinthians 14:19	52

1 Corinthians 14:20	54
1 Corinthians 14:21	56
1 Corinthians 14:22	58
1 Corinthians 14:23	60
1 Corinthians 14:24	62
Week 5 Prep Work	64
1 Corinthians 14:25	66
1 Corinthians 14:26	68
1 Corinthians 14:27	70
1 Corinthians 14:28	72
1 Corinthians 14:29	74
1 Corinthians 14:30	76
Week 6 Prep Work	78
1 Corinthians 14:31	80
1 Corinthians 14:32	82
1 Corinthians 14:33	84
1 Corinthians 14:34	86
1 Corinthians 14:35	88
1 Corinthians 14:36	90
Week 7 Prep Work	92
1 Corinthians 14:37	94
1 Corinthians 14:38	96
1 Corinthians 14:39	98
1 Corinthians 14:40	100
Conclusion	102

Before You Begin

Hey reader, before you begin memorizing scripture, I wanted to say thank you by offering a free gift.

I wrote a book called Memorize the Sermon on the Mount and I'd like to give you a free copy.

Simply text BIBLE to (678) 506-7543 and I'll send you a free copy straight to your inbox.

I've even thrown in a free bonus gift just for you.

I pray it becomes a blessing to you as you seal God's Word in your heart.

Introduction

I would like to start off by saying that I have prayed for you, whoever you are, wherever you are, as you are just beginning to start this journey to memorize a piece of the Bible.

In this book, you're going to memorize 1 Corinthians 14.

In 1 Corinthians 14, Paul is giving a close-up of two particular gifts of the Holy Spirit: prophecy and speaking in tongues. He urges the church members of Corinth that speak in tongues to be careful using their gift as to not confuse people who were not yet Christians. In public gatherings, prophecy was a better gift because others could learn from the message. The last section of the chapter deals with orderly worship that is respectable to each other and God.

At 40 verses long, it will take some work on your part to commit the passage to memory.

This is a game of repetition over time and this book will guide you every step of the way.

That said, there are no tricks, magic strategies, or brain hacks to make it work.

It just takes work but work that is incredibly rewarding.

INTRODUCTION

But even with all that said, there are probably excuses piling up in your head.

Little lies telling you a thousand reasons why you can't possibly remember a section of the Bible.

"I have a bad memory."

"I don't have enough time."

And many other reasons why you might tell yourself this won't work.

Memorizing a passage of the Bible can feel daunting but you don't need to start off by memorizing everything at once.

You just need to start with one verse.

And with that, you're ready to head to the next chapter to learn how to use this book.

How To Use This Book

By now you are probably curious how this book will work so I will quickly give you an overview.

This book covers the entire chapter of 1 Corinthians 14, English Standard Version.

This passage of scripture is broken down verse by verse and I recommend you memorize one verse each day working your way through memorizing the entire passage.

Each verse has one dedicated chapter and as mentioned before, this book uses the ESV (English Standard Version) translation. You will be guided to either repeat or recite a verse or verses during each chapter.

This book is set up so that you don't need to have your Bible in front of you to read from.

There are a handful of chapters, though optional, that are the weekly preparation chapters involving some optional prep work. This prep work will make memorizing the entire passage significantly easier and time well spent on your journey to memorizing God's Word. I highly recommend you do it, but feel free to skip it.

Also, I do not require you to say the verse number when memorizing scripture. The original scriptures were not numbered into verses so I don't believe that is a critical piece to remember. However, if you would like to state the verse number when reciting each verse, you are more than welcome to.

As you work your way through memorizing each verse, there will be days where you will get frustrated. It will seem the verse just won't stick. That is completely normal. Some verses will be significantly harder to memorize than others. That is okay. Don't be afraid to repeat a chapter if you feel you didn't quite memorize the verse that day.

If the first round of repetition didn't help it stick, the second or third round should surely do the trick.

You are ready to begin on a wonderful, spirit-filled journey to solidifying a piece of God's Word inside of your heart.

May it be an incredible blessing on your life and your personal walk with Christ.

Week 1 Prep Work

Welcome to the preparation work on your journey to memorizing 1 Corinthians 14.

Like I mentioned in the introduction, this work is completely optional, but I cannot encourage you enough to do the prep work.

If you had four hours to chop down a tree with a dull axe, you would be better off sharpening your axe for two of those four hours before getting started.

This prep work is sharpening your axe.

It will make everything moving forward significantly easier.

Though it will take time, this will be time well spent which you may not realize until you begin memorizing each verse one by one.

To complete the prep work, you will need to read the passage out loud 50 times.

Sounds daunting, doesn't it?

Reading out loud 1 Corinthians 14 would take roughly 7 minutes. Do that 50 times and you are looking at roughly 6 hours worth of reading out loud.

WEEK 1 PREP WORK

Not many people would have the luxury in spare time to squeeze that in and I'm not asking you to.

Instead of doing the entire passage in one go, you are going to do a smaller chunk that would allow you to accomplish the task in an hour or less.

You are going to focus on just the first six verses as you read them out loud 50 times.

Don't have an hour?

Do it for 30 minutes running through them 25 times.

Or commit to what you can. I assure you, whatever you do here will help.

Whenever you try to memorize something from scratch, it can feel like there is a lot of resistance to get the material to stick in your brain.

But if you are very familiar with whatever you are trying to commit to memory, it is like globbing memory glue on it before you get started.

After each week, you will have an opportunity to attempt the next block of 6 verses for the following week.

If you have decided to do the prep work, get ready to read the following chunk of verses out loud. Oh, and grab a glass of water. Your mouth can get pretty dry doing this prep work.

Please note, I left the verse numbers in the passage on the next page for your reference only.

When you are ready, begin.

1 Pursue love, and earnestly desire the spiritual gifts, especially that you may prophesy. 2 For one who speaks in a tongue speaks not to men but to God; for no one understands him, but he utters mysteries in the Spirit. 3 On the other hand, the one who prophesies speaks to people for their upbuilding and encouragement and consolation. 4 The one who speaks in a tongue builds up himself, but the one who prophesies builds up the church. 5 Now I want you all to speak in tongues, but even more to prophesy. The one who prophesies is greater than the one who speaks in tongues, unless someone interprets, so that the church may be built up. 6 Now, brothers, if I come to you speaking in tongues, how will I benefit you unless I bring you some revelation or knowledge or prophecy or teaching? (1 Corinthians 14:1-6 ESV)

See you tomorrow!

1 Corinthians 14:1

Today you are going to memorize 1 Corinthians 14:1.

You are going to memorize the verse by using the 10-10-10 method.

To use this method, each verse will be repeated out loud 10 times and then immediately recited 10 times from memory. In later chapters, you'll start combining verses and reciting those 10 times as well.

Don't worry if that was a little confusing to follow. Just follow the instructions and you will do just fine.

I understand 10 times may seem excessive and tedious, but trust me, this is necessary. There will be times where it may take you speaking a verse 5 times or more just to fully nail it down before being able to recite it from memory.

As a last word of advice before you begin, I wanted to share with you a few tips that have helped me memorize scripture:

1. Speaking the verse with conviction or emotion as you repeat or recite it from memory.
2. Emphasizing a different word each time you say it out loud.
3. Use hand motions as you speak.
4. Creating images in your head corresponding to each piece of a verse.

5. Singing a verse or a piece of a verse instead of speaking it.

Yes, you heard that last one right. It's weird, it works, but don't feel you need to incorporate all of these at once or any at all. As you go deeper into memorizing scripture, you will find what works for you and what doesn't.

Let's begin.

Say the following verse out loud ten times. You do not have to say the citation within the parenthesis.

"Pursue love, and earnestly desire the spiritual gifts, especially that you may prophesy" (1 Corinthians 14:1).

When you are done, recite the verse ten times in a row from memory, doing your best not to look at the verse.

Great job! You got your first verse down!

Throughout your day when you are driving your car, taking a break from work, or cooking a meal, go over what you've memorized so far to keep reinforcing it in your mind.

Tomorrow you'll quickly review what you learned today and add another verse to it.

If you don't feel confident you've truly memorized today's verse, consider going through the chapter again.

See you tomorrow!

God Bless.

1 Corinthians 14:2

Today you are going to memorize 1 Corinthians 14:2.

After you review what you have already learned, you are going to memorize today's verse using the 10-10-10 Method.

Let's begin.

Let's review the verse you learned yesterday by reciting it 10 times from memory. Glance over it if you need a refresher.

"Pursue love, and earnestly desire the spiritual gifts, especially that you may prophesy" (1 Corinthians 14:1).

When your review is done, let's get into today's verse.

Say the following verse out loud 10 times.

"For one who speaks in a tongue speaks not to men but to God; for no one understands him, but he utters mysteries in the Spirit" (1 Corinthians 14:2).

When you are done, recite the verse 10 times in a row from memory, doing your best not to look at the verse.

Great job! You got your next verse down!

You know the drill. Throughout your day when you're driving to work, taking a break from work, or cooking a meal, go over what you've memorized so far to keep reinforcing it in your mind.

Tomorrow you'll quickly review what you learned today and add another verse to it.

If you don't feel confident you've truly memorized today's verse, consider listening through the chapter again.

See you tomorrow!

Good Bless

1 Corinthians 14:3

Today you are going to memorize 1 Corinthians 14:3.

After you review what you have already learned, you are going to memorize today's verse using the 10-10-10 Method.

Let's begin.

Let's review the verse you learned yesterday by reciting it 10 times from memory. Glance over it if you need a refresher.

"For one who speaks in a tongue speaks not to men but to God; for no one understands him, but he utters mysteries in the Spirit" (1 Corinthians 14:2).

Now you're going to review all the verses you have memorized up to this point by reciting them 10 times. You can find it in the prep work chapter for this week if you need a refresher. If after three times you feel confident in your ability to recite all the verses you have currently memorized, feel free to call it good enough.

When your review is done, let's get into today's verse.

Say the following verse out loud 10 times:

"On the other hand, the one who prophesies speaks to people for their upbuilding and encouragement and consolation" (1 Corinthians 14:3).

When you are done, recite the verse 10 times in a row from memory, doing your best not to look at the verse.

Great job! You got your next verse down!

You know the drill, throughout your day when you're driving to work, taking a break from work, or cooking a meal, go over what you've memorized so far to keep reinforcing it in your mind.

Tomorrow you'll quickly review what you learned today and add another verse to it.

If you don't feel confident you've truly memorized today's verse, consider listening through the chapter again.

See you tomorrow!

God bless.

1 Corinthians 14:4

Today you are going to memorize 1 Corinthians 14:4.

After you review what you have already learned, you are going to memorize today's verse using the 10-10-10 Method.

Let's begin.

Let's review the verse you learned yesterday by reciting it 10 times from memory. Glance over it if you need a refresher.

"On the other hand, the one who prophesies speaks to people for their upbuilding and encouragement and consolation" (1 Corinthians 14:3).

Now you're going to review all the verses you have memorized up to this point by reciting them 10 times. You can find it in the prep work chapter for this week if you need a refresher. If after three times you feel confident in your ability to recite all the verses you have currently memorized, feel free to call it good enough.

When your review is done, let's get into today's verse.

Say the following verse out loud 10 times:

"The one who speaks in a tongue builds up himself, but the one who prophesies builds up the church" (1 Corinthians 14:4).

When you are done, recite the verse 10 times in a row from memory, doing your best not to look at the verse.

Great job! You got your next verse down!

You know the drill, throughout your day when you're driving to work, taking a break from work, or cooking a meal, go over what you've memorized so far to keep reinforcing it in your mind.

Tomorrow you'll quickly review what you learned today and add another verse to it.

If you don't feel confident you've truly memorized today's verse, consider listening through the chapter again.

See you tomorrow!
  God bless.

1 Corinthians 14:5

Today you are going to memorize 1 Corinthians 14:5.

After you review what you have already learned, you are going to memorize today's verse using the 10-10-10 Method.

Let's begin.

Let's review the verse you learned yesterday by reciting it 10 times from memory. Glance over it if you need a refresher.

"The one who speaks in a tongue builds up himself, but the one who prophesies builds up the church" (1 Corinthians 14:4).

Now you're going to review all the verses you have memorized up to this point by reciting them 10 times. You can find it in the prep work chapter for this week if you need a refresher. If after three times you feel confident in your ability to recite all the verses you have currently memorized, feel free to call it good enough.

When your review is done, let's get into today's verse.

Say the following verse out loud 10 times:

"Now I want you all to speak in tongues, but even more to prophesy. The one who prophesies is greater than the one who speaks in tongues, unless someone interprets, so that the church may be built up" (1 Corinthians 14:5).

When you are done, recite the verse 10 times in a row from memory, doing your best not to look at the verse.

Great job! You got your next verse down!

You know the drill, throughout your day when you're driving to work, taking a break from work, or cooking a meal, go over what you've memorized so far to keep reinforcing it in your mind.

Tomorrow you'll quickly review what you learned today and add another verse to it.

If you don't feel confident you've truly memorized today's verse, consider listening through the chapter again.

See you tomorrow!

God bless.

1 Corinthians 14:6

Today you are going to memorize 1 Corinthians 14:6.

After you review what you have already learned, you are going to memorize today's verse using the 10-10-10 Method.

Let's begin.

Let's review the verse you learned yesterday by reciting it 10 times from memory. Glance over it if you need a refresher.

"Now I want you all to speak in tongues, but even more to prophesy. The one who prophesies is greater than the one who speaks in tongues, unless someone interprets, so that the church may be built up" (1 Corinthians 14:5).

Now you're going to review all the verses you have memorized up to this point by reciting them 10 times. You can find it in the prep work chapter for this week if you need a refresher. If after three times you feel confident in your ability to recite all the verses you have currently memorized, feel free to call it good enough.

When your review is done, let's get into today's verse.

Say the following verse out loud 10 times:

"Now, brothers, if I come to you speaking in tongues, how will I benefit you unless I bring you some revelation or knowledge or prophecy or teaching?" (1 Corinthians 14:6).

When you are done, recite the verse 10 times in a row from memory, doing your best not to look at the verse.

Great job! You got your next verse down and your first block of 6 verses, too!

With your first block of verses completed, I would love to hear what you think so far about the book in the form of a review.

Reviews help other listeners find this book so that they too can become more intimate with God's Word.

Better yet, leaving a review is easy.

Simply go to the book's page on Amazon, scroll down and click the 'leave a customer review' button, choose a rating, leave a few words, and you're done!

Bonus points for leaving a picture with your review.

Super bonus points for a video.

Just a few minutes of your time will help people from all over the world, people you may never meet in this life, find this book and seal God's Word in their hearts.

Tomorrow you have the optional prep work for the next block of 6 verses. Though it's not mandatory, I can't stress enough how beneficial it will be moving forward.

If you plan to skip it, simply move to the following chapter to begin memorizing the first verse of the next block of 6 verses.

See you tomorrow!

God Bless!

Week 2 Prep Work

If you are here, that tells me you are ready for your next block of verses to memorize.

Great job so far. I know it takes a lot of time and effort to memorize scripture and I hope all that time and effort has been a joyful experience.

Just like with the first round of prep work, this is completely optional.

You are not required to do this to memorize the next block of 6 verses.

But like I said before, it will make the task much easier.

If you are not up for the prep work, feel free to skip this chapter.

If you are willing to give it a shot, get ready to read the next 6 verses out loud 50 times which will take you about an hour.

If you don't have an hour, run through them 25 times which will only take you about 30 minutes.

Or commit to whatever you can.

Anything and everything you do here will help moving forward.

WEEK 2 PREP WORK

Please note, I left the verse numbers in the passage for your reference only.

When you are ready, begin.

7 If even lifeless instruments, such as the flute or the harp, do not give distinct notes, how will anyone know what is played? 8 And if the bugle gives an indistinct sound, who will get ready for battle? 9 So with yourselves, if with your tongue you utter speech that is not intelligible, how will anyone know what is said? For you will be speaking into the air. 10 There are doubtless many different languages in the world, and none is without meaning, 11 but if I do not know the meaning of the language, I will be a foreigner to the speaker and the speaker a foreigner to me. 12 So with yourselves, since you are eager for manifestations of the Spirit, strive to excel in building up the church. (1 Corinthians 14:7-12)

See you tomorrow!

1 Corinthians 14:7

Today you are going to memorize 1 Corinthians 14:7.

After you review what you have already learned, you are going to memorize today's verse using the 10-10-10 Method.

Let's begin.

Let's review the verse you learned last by reciting it 10 times from memory. Glance over it if you need a refresher.

"Now, brothers, if I come to you speaking in tongues, how will I benefit you unless I bring you some revelation or knowledge or prophecy or teaching?" (1 Corinthians 14:6).

Now you're going to review all the verses you have memorized up to this point by reciting them 10 times. You can find it in the prep work chapter for this week if you need a refresher. If after three times you feel confident in your ability to recite all the verses you have currently memorized, feel free to call it good enough.

When your review is done, let's get into today's verse.

Say the following verse out loud 10 times:

"If even lifeless instruments, such as the flute or the harp, do not give distinct notes, how will anyone know what is played?" (1 Corinthians 14:7).

When you are done, recite the verse 10 times in a row from memory, doing your best not to look at the verse.

Great job! You got your next verse down!

You know the drill, throughout your day when you're driving to work, taking a break from work, or cooking a meal, go over what you've memorized so far to keep reinforcing it in your mind.

Tomorrow you'll quickly review what you learned today and add another verse to it.

If you don't feel confident you've truly memorized today's verse, consider listening through the chapter again.

See you tomorrow!

God bless.

1 Corinthians 14:8

Today you are going to memorize 1 Corinthians 14:8.

After you review what you have already learned, you are going to memorize today's verse using the 10-10-10 Method.

Let's begin.

Let's review the verse you learned yesterday by reciting it 10 times from memory. Glance over it if you need a refresher.

"If even lifeless instruments, such as the flute or the harp, do not give distinct notes, how will anyone know what is played?" (1 Corinthians 14:7).

Now you're going to review all the verses you have memorized up to this point by reciting them 10 times. You can find it in the prep work chapter for this week if you need a refresher. If after three times you feel confident in your ability to recite all the verses you have currently memorized, feel free to call it good enough.

When your review is done, let's get into today's verse.

Say the following verse out loud 10 times:

"And if the bugle gives an indistinct sound, who will get ready for battle?"
(1 Corinthians 14:8).

When you are done, recite the verse 10 times in a row from memory, doing your best not to look at the verse.

Great job! You got your next verse down!

You know the drill, throughout your day when you're driving to work, taking a break from work, or cooking a meal, go over what you've memorized so far to keep reinforcing it in your mind.

Tomorrow you'll quickly review what you learned today and add another verse to it.

If you don't feel confident you've truly memorized today's verse, consider listening through the chapter again.

See you tomorrow!

God bless.

1 Corinthians 14:9

Today you are going to memorize 1 Corinthians 14:9.

After you review what you have already learned, you are going to memorize today's verse using the 10-10-10 Method.

Let's begin.

Let's review the verse you learned yesterday by reciting it 10 times from memory. Glance over it if you need a refresher.

"And if the bugle gives an indistinct sound, who will get ready for battle?" (1 Corinthians 14:8).

Now you're going to review all the verses you have memorized up to this point by reciting them 10 times. You can find it in the prep work chapter for this week if you need a refresher. If after three times you feel confident in your ability to recite all the verses you have currently memorized, feel free to call it good enough.

When your review is done, let's get into today's verse.

Say the following verse out loud 10 times:

"So with yourselves, if with your tongue you utter speech that is not intelligible, how will anyone know what is said? For you will be speaking into the air" (1 Corinthians 14:9).

When you are done, recite the verse 10 times in a row from memory, doing your best not to look at the verse.

Great job! You got your next verse down!

You know the drill, throughout your day when you're driving to work, taking a break from work, or cooking a meal, go over what you've memorized so far to keep reinforcing it in your mind.

Tomorrow you'll quickly review what you learned today and add another verse to it.

If you don't feel confident you've truly memorized today's verse, consider listening through the chapter again.

See you tomorrow!

God bless.

1 Corinthians 14:10

Today you are going to memorize 1 Corinthians 14:10.

After you review what you have already learned, you are going to memorize today's verse using the 10-10-10 Method.

Let's begin.

Let's review the verse you learned yesterday by reciting it 10 times from memory. Glance over it if you need a refresher.

"So with yourselves, if with your tongue you utter speech that is not intelligible, how will anyone know what is said? For you will be speaking into the air" (1 Corinthians 14:9).

Now you're going to review all the verses you have memorized up to this point by reciting them 10 times. You can find it in the prep work chapter for this week if you need a refresher. If after three times you feel confident in your ability to recite all the verses you have currently memorized, feel free to call it good enough.

When your review is done, let's get into today's verse.

Say the following verse out loud 10 times:

"There are doubtless many different languages in the world, and none is without meaning" (1 Corinthians 14:10).

When you are done, recite the verse 10 times in a row from memory, doing your best not to look at the verse.

Great job! You got your next verse down!

You know the drill, throughout your day when you're driving to work, taking a break from work, or cooking a meal, go over what you've memorized so far to keep reinforcing it in your mind.

Tomorrow you'll quickly review what you learned today and add another verse to it.

If you don't feel confident you've truly memorized today's verse, consider listening through the chapter again.

See you tomorrow!

God bless.

1 Corinthians 14:11

Today you are going to memorize 1 Corinthians 14:11.

After you review what you have already learned, you are going to memorize today's verse using the 10-10-10 Method.

Let's begin.

Let's review the verse you learned yesterday by reciting it 10 times from memory. Glance over it if you need a refresher.

"There are doubtless many different languages in the world, and none is without meaning" (1 Corinthians 14:10).

Now you're going to review all the verses you have memorized up to this point by reciting them 10 times. You can find it in the prep work chapter for this week if you need a refresher. If after three times you feel confident in your ability to recite all the verses you have currently memorized, feel free to call it good enough.

When your review is done, let's get into today's verse.

Say the following verse out loud 10 times:

"But if I do not know the meaning of the language, I will be a foreigner to the speaker and the speaker a foreigner to me" (1 Corinthians 14:11).

When you are done, recite the verse 10 times in a row from memory, doing your best not to look at the verse.

Great job! You got your next verse down!

You know the drill, throughout your day when you're driving to work, taking a break from work, or cooking a meal, go over what you've memorized so far to keep reinforcing it in your mind.

Tomorrow you'll quickly review what you learned today and add another verse to it.

If you don't feel confident you've truly memorized today's verse, consider listening through the chapter again.

See you tomorrow!

God bless.

1 Corinthians 14:12

Today you are going to memorize 1 Corinthians 14:12.

After you review what you have already learned, you are going to memorize today's verse using the 10-10-10 Method.

Let's begin.

Let's review the verse you learned yesterday by reciting it 10 times from memory. Glance over it if you need a refresher.

"But if I do not know the meaning of the language, I will be a foreigner to the speaker and the speaker a foreigner to me" (1 Corinthians 14:11).

Now you're going to review all the verses you have memorized up to this point by reciting them 10 times. You can find it in the prep work chapter for this week if you need a refresher. If after three times you feel confident in your ability to recite all the verses you have currently memorized, feel free to call it good enough.

When your review is done, let's get into today's verse.

Say the following verse out loud 10 times:

"So with yourselves, since you are eager for manifestations of the Spirit, strive to excel in building up the church" (1 Corinthians 14:12).

When you are done, recite the verse 10 times in a row from memory, doing your best not to look at the verse.

Great job! You got your next verse down!

You know the drill, throughout your day when you're driving to work, taking a break from work, or cooking a meal, go over what you've memorized so far to keep reinforcing it in your mind.

Tomorrow you have the optional prep work for the next block of 6 verses. Though it's not mandatory, I can't stress enough how beneficial it will be moving forward.

If you plan to skip it, simply move to the following chapter to begin memorizing the first verse of the next block of 6 verses.

If you don't feel confident you've truly memorized today's verse, consider listening through the chapter again.

See you tomorrow!

God bless.

Week 3 Prep Work

If you are here, that tells me you are ready for your next block of verses to memorize.

Great job so far. I know it takes a lot of time and effort to memorize scripture and I hope all that time and effort has been a joyful experience.

Just like with the first round of prep work, this is completely optional.

You are not required to do this to memorize the next block of 6 verses.

But like I said before, it will make the task much easier.

If you are not up for the prep work, feel free to skip this chapter.

If you are willing to give it a shot, get ready to read the next 6 verses out loud 50 times which will take you about an hour.

If you don't have an hour, run through them 25 times which will only take you about 30 minutes.

Or commit to whatever you can.

Anything and everything you do here will help moving forward.

WEEK 3 PREP WORK

Please note, I left the verse numbers in the passage for your reference only.

When you are ready, begin.

13 Therefore, one who speaks in a tongue should pray that he may interpret. 14 For if I pray in a tongue, my spirit prays but my mind is unfruitful. 15 What am I to do? I will pray with my spirit, but I will pray with my mind also; I will sing praise with my spirit, but I will sing with my mind also. 16 Otherwise, if you give thanks with your spirit, how can anyone in the position of an outsider say "Amen" to your thanksgiving when he does not know what you are saying? 17 For you may be giving thanks well enough, but the other person is not being built up. 18 I thank God that I speak in tongues more than all of you. (1 Corinthians 14:13-18)

See you tomorrow!

1 Corinthians 14:13

Today you are going to memorize 1 Corinthians 14:13.

After you review what you have already learned, you are going to memorize today's verse using the 10-10-10 Method.

Let's begin.

Let's review the verse you learned yesterday by reciting it 10 times from memory. Glance over it if you need a refresher.

"So with yourselves, since you are eager for manifestations of the Spirit, strive to excel in building up the church" (1 Corinthians 14:12).

Now you're going to review all the verses you have memorized up to this point by reciting them 10 times. You can find it in the prep work chapter for this week if you need a refresher. If after three times you feel confident in your ability to recite all the verses you have currently memorized, feel free to call it good enough.

When your review is done, let's get into today's verse.

Say the following verse out loud 10 times:

"Therefore, one who speaks in a tongue should pray that he may interpret" (1 Corinthians 14:13).

When you are done, recite the verse 10 times in a row from memory, doing your best not to look at the verse.

Great job! You got your next verse down!

You know the drill, throughout your day when you're driving to work, taking a break from work, or cooking a meal, go over what you've memorized so far to keep reinforcing it in your mind.

Tomorrow you'll quickly review what you learned today and add another verse to it.

If you don't feel confident you've truly memorized today's verse, consider listening through the chapter again.

See you tomorrow!

God bless.

1 Corinthians 14:14

Today you are going to memorize 1 Corinthians 14:14.

After you review what you have already learned, you are going to memorize today's verse using the 10-10-10 Method.

Let's begin.

Let's review the verse you learned last by reciting it 10 times from memory. Glance over it if you need a refresher.

"Therefore, one who speaks in a tongue should pray that he may interpret" (1 Corinthians 14:13).

Now you're going to review all the verses you have memorized up to this point by reciting them 10 times. You can find it in the prep work chapter for this week if you need a refresher. If after three times you feel confident in your ability to recite all the verses you have currently memorized, feel free to call it good enough.

When your review is done, let's get into today's verse.

Say the following verse out loud 10 times:

"For if I pray in a tongue, my spirit prays but my mind is unfruitful" (1 Corinthians 14:14).

When you are done, recite the verse 10 times in a row from memory, doing your best not to look at the verse.

Great job! You got your next verse down!

You know the drill, throughout your day when you're driving to work, taking a break from work, or cooking a meal, go over what you've memorized so far to keep reinforcing it in your mind.

Tomorrow you'll quickly review what you learned today and add another verse to it.

If you don't feel confident you've truly memorized today's verse, consider listening through the chapter again.

See you tomorrow!

God bless.

1 Corinthians 14:15

Today you are going to memorize 1 Corinthians 14:15.

After you review what you have already learned, you are going to memorize today's verse using the 10-10-10 Method.

Let's begin.

Let's review the verse you learned yesterday by reciting it 10 times from memory. Glance over it if you need a refresher.

"For if I pray in a tongue, my spirit prays but my mind is unfruitful" (1 Corinthians 14:14).

Now you're going to review all the verses you have memorized up to this point by reciting them 10 times. You can find it in the prep work chapter for this week if you need a refresher. If after three times you feel confident in your ability to recite all the verses you have currently memorized, feel free to call it good enough.

When your review is done, let's get into today's verse.

Say the following verse out loud 10 times:

"What am I to do? I will pray with my spirit, but I will pray with my mind also; I will sing praise with my spirit, but I will sing with my mind also" (1 Corinthians 14:15).

When you are done, recite the verse 10 times in a row from memory, doing your best not to look at the verse.

Great job! You got your next verse down!

You know the drill, throughout your day when you're driving to work, taking a break from work, or cooking a meal, go over what you've memorized so far to keep reinforcing it in your mind.

Tomorrow you'll quickly review what you learned today and add another verse to it.

If you don't feel confident you've truly memorized today's verse, consider listening through the chapter again.

See you tomorrow!

God bless.

1 Corinthians 14:16

Today you are going to memorize 1 Corinthians 14:16.

After you review what you have already learned, you are going to memorize today's verse using the 10-10-10 Method.

Let's begin.

Let's review the verse you learned yesterday by reciting it 10 times from memory. Glance over it if you need a refresher.

"What am I to do? I will pray with my spirit, but I will pray with my mind also; I will sing praise with my spirit, but I will sing with my mind also" (1 Corinthians 14:15).

Now you're going to review all the verses you have memorized up to this point by reciting them 10 times. You can find it in the prep work chapter for this week if you need a refresher. If after three times you feel confident in your ability to recite all the verses you have currently memorized, feel free to call it good enough.

When your review is done, let's get into today's verse.

Say the following verse out loud 10 times:

1 CORINTHIANS 14:16

"Otherwise, if you give thanks with your spirit, how can anyone in the position of an outsider say 'Amen' to your thanksgiving when he does not know what you are saying?" (1 Corinthians 14:16).

When you are done, recite the verse 10 times in a row from memory, doing your best not to look at the verse.

Great job! You got your next verse down!

You know the drill, throughout your day when you're driving to work, taking a break from work, or cooking a meal, go over what you've memorized so far to keep reinforcing it in your mind.

Tomorrow you'll quickly review what you learned today and add another verse to it.

If you don't feel confident you've truly memorized today's verse, consider listening through the chapter again.

See you tomorrow!

God bless.

1 Corinthians 14:17

Today you are going to memorize 1 Corinthians 14:17.

After you review what you have already learned, you are going to memorize today's verse using the 10-10-10 Method.

Let's begin.

Let's review the verse you learned yesterday by reciting it 10 times from memory. Glance over it if you need a refresher.

"Otherwise, if you give thanks with your spirit, how can anyone in the position of an outsider say 'Amen' to your thanksgiving when he does not know what you are saying?" (1 Corinthians 14:16).

Now you're going to review all the verses you have memorized up to this point by reciting them 10 times. You can find it in the prep work chapter for this week if you need a refresher. If after three times you feel confident in your ability to recite all the verses you have currently memorized, feel free to call it good enough.

When your review is done, let's get into today's verse.

Say the following verse out loud 10 times:

"For you may be giving thanks well enough, but the other person is not being built up" (1 Corinthians 14:17).

When you are done, recite the verse 10 times in a row from memory, doing your best not to look at the verse.

Great job! You got your next verse down!

You know the drill, throughout your day when you're driving to work, taking a break from work, or cooking a meal, go over what you've memorized so far to keep reinforcing it in your mind.

Tomorrow you'll quickly review what you learned today and add another verse to it.

If you don't feel confident you've truly memorized today's verse, consider listening through the chapter again.

See you tomorrow!

God bless.

1 Corinthians 14:18

Today you are going to memorize 1 Corinthians 14:18.

After you review what you have already learned, you are going to memorize today's verse using the 10-10-10 Method.

Let's begin.

Let's review the verse you learned yesterday by reciting it 10 times from memory. Glance over it if you need a refresher.

"For you may be giving thanks well enough, but the other person is not being built up" (1 Corinthians 14:17).

Now you're going to review all the verses you have memorized up to this point by reciting them 10 times. You can find it in the prep work chapter for this week if you need a refresher. If after three times you feel confident in your ability to recite all the verses you have currently memorized, feel free to call it good enough.

When your review is done, let's get into today's verse.

Say the following verse out loud 10 times:

"I thank God that I speak in tongues more than all of you" (1 Corinthians 14:18).

When you are done, recite the verse 10 times in a row from memory, doing your best not to look at the verse.

Great job! You got your next verse down!

You know the drill, throughout your day when you're driving to work, taking a break from work, or cooking a meal, go over what you've memorized so far to keep reinforcing it in your mind.

Tomorrow you have the optional prep work for the next block of 6 verses. Though it's not mandatory, I can't stress enough how beneficial it will be moving forward.

If you plan to skip it, simply move to the following chapter to begin memorizing the first verse of the next block of 6 verses.

If you don't feel confident you've truly memorized today's verse, consider listening through the chapter again.

See you tomorrow!

God bless.

Week 4 Prep Work

If you are here, that tells me you are ready for your next block of verses to memorize.

Great job so far. I know it takes a lot of time and effort to memorize scripture and I hope all that time and effort has been a joyful experience.

Just like with the first round of prep work, this is completely optional.

You are not required to do this to memorize the next block of 6 verses.

But like I said before, it will make the task much easier.

If you are not up for the prep work, feel free to skip this chapter.

If you are willing to give it a shot, get ready to read the next 6 verses out loud 50 times which will take you about an hour.

If you don't have an hour, run through them 25 times which will only take you about 30 minutes.

Or commit to whatever you can.

Anything and everything you do here will help moving forward.

Please note, I left the verse numbers in the passage for your reference only.

When you are ready, begin.

19 Nevertheless, in church I would rather speak five words with my mind in order to instruct others, than ten thousand words in a tongue. 20 Brothers, do not be children in your thinking. Be infants in evil, but in your thinking be mature. 21 In the Law it is written, "By people of strange tongues and by the lips of foreigners will I speak to this people, and even then they will not listen to me, says the Lord." 22 Thus tongues are a sign not for believers but for unbelievers, while prophecy is a sign not for unbelievers but for believers. 23 If, therefore, the whole church comes together and all speak in tongues, and outsiders or unbelievers enter, will they not say that you are out of your minds? 24 But if all prophesy, and an unbeliever or outsider enters, he is convicted by all, he is called to account by all. (1 Corinthians 14:19-24)

See you tomorrow!

1 Corinthians 14:19

Today you are going to memorize 1 Corinthians 14:19.

After you review what you have already learned, you are going to memorize today's verse using the 10-10-10 Method.

Let's begin.

Let's review the verse you learned yesterday by reciting it 10 times from memory. Glance over it if you need a refresher.

"I thank God that I speak in tongues more than all of you" (1 Corinthians 14:18).

Now you're going to review all the verses you have memorized up to this point by reciting them 10 times. You can find it in the prep work chapter for this week if you need a refresher. If after three times you feel confident in your ability to recite all the verses you have currently memorized, feel free to call it good enough.

When your review is done, let's get into today's verse.

Say the following verse out loud 10 times:

"Nevertheless, in church I would rather speak five words with my mind in order to instruct others, than ten thousand words in a tongue" (1 Corinthians 14:19).

When you are done, recite the verse 10 times in a row from memory, doing your best not to look at the verse.

Great job! You got your next verse down!

You know the drill, throughout your day when you're driving to work, taking a break from work, or cooking a meal, go over what you've memorized so far to keep reinforcing it in your mind.

Tomorrow you'll quickly review what you learned today and add another verse to it.

If you don't feel confident you've truly memorized today's verse, consider listening through the chapter again.

See you tomorrow!

God bless.

1 Corinthians 14:20

Today you are going to memorize 1 Corinthians 14:20.

After you review what you have already learned, you are going to memorize today's verse using the 10-10-10 Method.

Let's begin.

Let's review the verse you learned yesterday by reciting it 10 times from memory. Glance over it if you need a refresher.

"Nevertheless, in church I would rather speak five words with my mind in order to instruct others, than ten thousand words in a tongue" (1 Corinthians 14:19).

Now you're going to review all the verses you have memorized up to this point by reciting them 10 times. You can find it in the prep work chapter for this week if you need a refresher. If after three times you feel confident in your ability to recite all the verses you have currently memorized, feel free to call it good enough.

When your review is done, let's get into today's verse.

Say the following verse out loud 10 times:

"Brothers, do not be children in your thinking. Be infants in evil, but in your thinking be mature" (1 Corinthians 14:20).

When you are done, recite the verse 10 times in a row from memory, doing your best not to look at the verse.

Great job! You got your next verse down!

You know the drill, throughout your day when you're driving to work, taking a break from work, or cooking a meal, go over what you've memorized so far to keep reinforcing it in your mind.

Tomorrow you'll quickly review what you learned today and add another verse to it.

If you don't feel confident you've truly memorized today's verse, consider listening through the chapter again.

See you tomorrow!

God bless!

1 Corinthians 14:21

Today you are going to memorize 1 Corinthians 14:21.

After you review what you have already learned, you are going to memorize today's verse using the 10-10-10 Method.

Let's begin.

Let's review the verse you learned yesterday by reciting it 10 times from memory. Glance over it if you need a refresher.

"Brothers, do not be children in your thinking. Be infants in evil, but in your thinking be mature" (1 Corinthians 14:20).

Now you're going to review all the verses you have memorized up to this point by reciting them 10 times. You can find it in the prep work chapter for this week if you need a refresher. If after three times you feel confident in your ability to recite all the verses you have currently memorized, feel free to call it good enough.

When your review is done, let's get into today's verse.

Say the following verse out loud 10 times:

"In the Law it is written, 'By people of strange tongues and by the lips of foreigners will I speak to this people, and even then they will not listen to me, says the Lord'" (1 Corinthians 14:21).

When you are done, recite the verse 10 times in a row from memory, doing your best not to look at the verse.

Great job! You got your next verse down!

You know the drill, throughout your day when you're driving to work, taking a break from work, or cooking a meal, go over what you've memorized so far to keep reinforcing it in your mind.

Tomorrow you'll quickly review what you learned today and add another verse to it.

If you don't feel confident you've truly memorized today's verse, consider listening through the chapter again.

See you tomorrow!

God bless!

1 Corinthians 14:22

Today you are going to memorize 1 Corinthians 14:22.

After you review what you have already learned, you are going to memorize today's verse using the 10-10-10 Method.

Let's begin.

Let's review the verse you learned yesterday by reciting it 10 times from memory. Glance over it if you need a refresher.

"In the Law it is written, 'By people of strange tongues and by the lips of foreigners will I speak to this people, and even then they will not listen to me, says the Lord'" (1 Corinthians 14:21).

Now you're going to review all the verses you have memorized up to this point by reciting them 10 times. You can find it in the prep work chapter for this week if you need a refresher. If after three times you feel confident in your ability to recite all the verses you have currently memorized, feel free to call it good enough.

When your review is done, let's get into today's verse.

Say the following verse out loud 10 times:

"Thus tongues are a sign not for believers but for unbelievers, while prophecy is a sign not for unbelievers but for believers" (1 Corinthians 14:22).

When you are done, recite the verse 10 times in a row from memory, doing your best not to look at the verse.

Great job! You got your next verse down!

You know the drill, throughout your day when you're driving to work, taking a break from work, or cooking a meal, go over what you've memorized so far to keep reinforcing it in your mind.

Tomorrow you'll quickly review what you learned today and add another verse to it.

If you don't feel confident you've truly memorized today's verse, consider listening through the chapter again.

See you tomorrow!

God bless!

1 Corinthians 14:23

Today you are going to memorize 1 Corinthians 14:23.

After you review what you have already learned, you are going to memorize today's verse using the 10-10-10 Method.

Let's begin.

Let's review the verse you learned yesterday by reciting it 10 times from memory. Glance over it if you need a refresher.

"Thus tongues are a sign not for believers but for unbelievers, while prophecy is a sign not for unbelievers but for believers" (1 Corinthians 14:22).

Now you're going to review all the verses you have memorized up to this point by reciting them 10 times. You can find it in the prep work chapter for this week if you need a refresher. If after three times you feel confident in your ability to recite all the verses you have currently memorized, feel free to call it good enough.

When your review is done, let's get into today's verse.

Say the following verse out loud 10 times:

"If, therefore, the whole church comes together and all speak in tongues, and outsiders or unbelievers enter, will they not say that you are out of your minds?" (1 Corinthians 14:23).

When you are done, recite the verse 10 times in a row from memory, doing your best not to look at the verse.

Great job! You got your next verse down!

You know the drill, throughout your day when you're driving to work, taking a break from work, or cooking a meal, go over what you've memorized so far to keep reinforcing it in your mind.

Tomorrow you'll quickly review what you learned today and add another verse to it.

If you don't feel confident you've truly memorized today's verse, consider listening through the chapter again.

See you tomorrow!

God bless.

1 Corinthians 14:24

Today you are going to memorize 1 Corinthians 14:24.

After you review what you have already learned, you are going to memorize today's verse using the 10-10-10 Method.

Let's begin.

Let's review the verse you learned yesterday by reciting it 10 times from memory. Glance over it if you need a refresher.

"If, therefore, the whole church comes together and all speak in tongues, and outsiders or unbelievers enter, will they not say that you are out of your minds?" (1 Corinthians 14:23).

Now you're going to review all the verses you have memorized up to this point by reciting them 10 times. You can find it in the prep work chapter for this week if you need a refresher. If after three times you feel confident in your ability to recite all the verses you have currently memorized, feel free to call it good enough.

When your review is done, let's get into today's verse.

Say the following verse out loud 10 times:

"But if all prophesy, and an unbeliever or outsider enters, he is convicted by all, he is called to account by all" (1 Corinthians 14:24).

When you are done, recite the verse 10 times in a row from memory, doing your best not to look at the verse.

Great job! You got your next verse down!

You know the drill, throughout your day when you're driving to work, taking a break from work, or cooking a meal, go over what you've memorized so far to keep reinforcing it in your mind.

Tomorrow you have the optional prep work for the next block of 6 verses. Though it's not mandatory, I can't stress enough how beneficial it will be moving forward.

If you plan to skip it, simply move to the following chapter to begin memorizing the first verse of the next block of 6 verses.

If you don't feel confident you've truly memorized today's verse, consider listening through the chapter again.

See you tomorrow!

God bless.

Week 5 Prep Work

If you are here, that tells me you are ready for your next block of verses to memorize.

Great job so far. I know it takes a lot of time and effort to memorize scripture and I hope all that time and effort has been a joyful experience.

Just like with the first round of prep work, this is completely optional.

You are not required to do this to memorize the next block of 6 verses.

But like I said before, it will make the task much easier.

If you are not up for the prep work, feel free to skip this chapter.

If you are willing to give it a shot, get ready to read the next 6 verses out loud 50 times which will take you about an hour.

If you don't have an hour, run through them 25 times which will only take you about 30 minutes.

Or commit to whatever you can.

Anything and everything you do here will help moving forward.

Please note, I left the verse numbers in the passage for your reference only.

When you are ready, begin.

25 The secrets of his heart are disclosed, and so, falling on his face, he will worship God and declare that God is really among you. 26 What then, brothers? When you come together, each one has a hymn, a lesson, a revelation, a tongue, or an interpretation. Let all things be done for building up. 27 If any speak in a tongue, let there be only two or at most three, and each in turn, and let someone interpret. 28 But if there is no one to interpret, let each of them keep silent in church and speak to himself and to God. 29 Let two or three prophets speak, and let the others weigh what is said. 30 If a revelation is made to another sitting there, let the first be silent.
   (1 Corinthians 14:25-30)

See you tomorrow!

1 Corinthians 14:25

Today you are going to memorize 1 Corinthians 14:25.

After you review what you have already learned, you are going to memorize today's verse using the 10-10-10 Method.

Let's begin.

Let's review the verse you learned yesterday by reciting it 10 times from memory. Glance over it if you need a refresher.

"But if all prophesy, and an unbeliever or outsider enters, he is convicted by all, he is called to account by all" (1 Corinthians 14:24).

Now you're going to review all the verses you have memorized up to this point by reciting them 10 times. You can find it in the prep work chapter for this week if you need a refresher. If after three times you feel confident in your ability to recite all the verses you have currently memorized, feel free to call it good enough.

When your review is done, let's get into today's verse.

Say the following verse out loud 10 times:

"The secrets of his heart are disclosed, and so, falling on his face, he will worship God and declare that God is really among you" (1 Corinthians 14:25).

When you are done, recite the verse 10 times in a row from memory, doing your best not to look at the verse.

Great job! You got your next verse down!

You know the drill, throughout your day when you're driving to work, taking a break from work, or cooking a meal, go over what you've memorized so far to keep reinforcing it in your mind.

Tomorrow you'll quickly review what you learned today and add another verse to it.

If you don't feel confident you've truly memorized today's verse, consider listening through the chapter again.

See you tomorrow!

God bless.

1 Corinthians 14:26

Today you are going to memorize 1 Corinthians 14:26.

After you review what you have already learned, you are going to memorize today's verse using the 10-10-10 Method.

Let's begin.

Let's review the verse you learned yesterday by reciting it 10 times from memory. Glance over it if you need a refresher.

"The secrets of his heart are disclosed, and so, falling on his face, he will worship God and declare that God is really among you" (1 Corinthians 14:25).

Now you're going to review all the verses you have memorized up to this point by reciting them 10 times. You can find it in the prep work chapter for this week if you need a refresher. If after three times you feel confident in your ability to recite all the verses you have currently memorized, feel free to call it good enough.

When your review is done, let's get into today's verse.

Say the following verse out loud 10 times:

"What then, brothers? When you come together, each one has a hymn, a lesson, a revelation, a tongue, or an interpretation. Let all things be done for building up" (1 Corinthians 14:26).

When you are done, recite the verse 10 times in a row from memory, doing your best not to look at the verse.

Great job! You got your next verse down!

You know the drill, throughout your day when you're driving to work, taking a break from work, or cooking a meal, go over what you've memorized so far to keep reinforcing it in your mind.

Tomorrow you'll quickly review what you learned today and add another verse to it.

If you don't feel confident you've truly memorized today's verse, consider listening through the chapter again.

See you tomorrow!

God bless.

1 Corinthians 14:27

Today you are going to memorize 1 Corinthians 14:27.

After you review what you have already learned, you are going to memorize today's verse using the 10-10-10 Method.

Let's begin.

Let's review the verse you learned yesterday by reciting it 10 times from memory. Glance over it if you need a refresher.

"What then, brothers? When you come together, each one has a hymn, a lesson, a revelation, a tongue, or an interpretation. Let all things be done for building up" (1 Corinthians 14:26).

Now you're going to review all the verses you have memorized up to this point by reciting them 10 times. You can find it in the prep work chapter for this week if you need a refresher. If after three times you feel confident in your ability to recite all the verses you have currently memorized, feel free to call it good enough.

When your review is done, let's get into today's verse.

Say the following verse out loud 10 times:

"If any speak in a tongue, let there be only two or at most three, and each in turn, and let someone interpret" (1 Corinthians 14:27).

When you are done, recite the verse 10 times in a row from memory, doing your best not to look at the verse.

Great job! You got your next verse down!

You know the drill, throughout your day when you're driving to work, taking a break from work, or cooking a meal, go over what you've memorized so far to keep reinforcing it in your mind.

Tomorrow you'll quickly review what you learned today and add another verse to it.

If you don't feel confident you've truly memorized today's verse, consider listening through the chapter again.

See you tomorrow!

God bless!

1 Corinthians 14:28

Today you are going to memorize 1 Corinthians 14:28.

After you review what you have already learned, you are going to memorize today's verse using the 10-10-10 Method.

Let's begin.

Let's review the verse you learned yesterday by reciting it 10 times from memory. Glance over it if you need a refresher.

"If any speak in a tongue, let there be only two or at most three, and each in turn, and let someone interpret" (1 Corinthians 14:27).

Now you're going to review all the verses you have memorized up to this point by reciting them 10 times. You can find it in the prep work chapter for this week if you need a refresher. If after three times you feel confident in your ability to recite all the verses you have currently memorized, feel free to call it good enough.

When your review is done, let's get into today's verse.

Say the following verse out loud 10 times:

"But if there is no one to interpret, let each of them keep silent in church and speak to himself and to God" (1 Corinthians 14:28).

When you are done, recite the verse 10 times in a row from memory, doing your best not to look at the verse.

Great job! You got your next verse down!

You know the drill, throughout your day when you're driving to work, taking a break from work, or cooking a meal, go over what you've memorized so far to keep reinforcing it in your mind.

Tomorrow you'll quickly review what you learned today and add another verse to it.

If you don't feel confident you've truly memorized today's verse, consider listening through the chapter again.

See you tomorrow!

God bless!

1 Corinthians 14:29

Today you are going to memorize 1 Corinthians 14:29.

After you review what you have already learned, you are going to memorize today's verse using the 10-10-10 Method.

Let's begin.

Let's review the verse you learned yesterday by reciting it 10 times from memory. Glance over it if you need a refresher.

"But if there is no one to interpret, let each of them keep silent in church and speak to himself and to God" (1 Corinthians 14:28).

Now you're going to review all the verses you have memorized up to this point by reciting them 10 times. You can find it in the prep work chapter for this week if you need a refresher. If after three times you feel confident in your ability to recite all the verses you have currently memorized, feel free to call it good enough.

When your review is done, let's get into today's verse.

Say the following verse out loud 10 times:

"Let two or three prophets speak, and let the others weigh what is said" (1 Corinthians 14:29).

When you are done, recite the verse 10 times in a row from memory, doing your best not to look at the verse.

Great job! You got your next verse down!

You know the drill, throughout your day when you're driving to work, taking a break from work, or cooking a meal, go over what you've memorized so far to keep reinforcing it in your mind.

Tomorrow you'll quickly review what you learned today and add another verse to it.

If you don't feel confident you've truly memorized today's verse, consider listening through the chapter again.

See you tomorrow!

God bless!

1 Corinthians 14:30

Today you are going to memorize 1 Corinthians 14:30.

After you review what you have already learned, you are going to memorize today's verse using the 10-10-10 Method.

Let's begin.

Let's review the verse you learned yesterday by reciting it 10 times from memory. Glance over it if you need a refresher.

"Let two or three prophets speak, and let the others weigh what is said" (1 Corinthians 14:29).

Now you're going to review all the verses you have memorized up to this point by reciting them 10 times. You can find it in the prep work chapter for this week if you need a refresher. If after three times you feel confident in your ability to recite all the verses you have currently memorized, feel free to call it good enough.

When your review is done, let's get into today's verse.

Say the following verse out loud 10 times:

"If a revelation is made to another sitting there, let the first be silent" (1 Corinthians 14:30).

When you are done, recite the verse 10 times in a row from memory, doing your best not to look at the verse.

Great job! You got your next verse down!

You know the drill, throughout your day when you're driving to work, taking a break from work, or cooking a meal, go over what you've memorized so far to keep reinforcing it in your mind.

Tomorrow you have the optional prep work for the next block of 6 verses. Though it's not mandatory, I can't stress enough how beneficial it will be moving forward.

If you plan to skip it, simply move to the following chapter to begin memorizing the first verse of the next block of 6 verses.

If you don't feel confident you've truly memorized today's verse, consider listening through the chapter again.

See you tomorrow!

God bless.

Week 6 Prep Work

If you are here, that tells me you are ready for your next block of verses to memorize.

Great job so far. I know it takes a lot of time and effort to memorize scripture and I hope all that time and effort has been a joyful experience.

Just like with the first round of prep work, this is completely optional.

You are not required to do this to memorize the next block of 6 verses.

But like I said before, it will make the task much easier.

If you are not up for the prep work, feel free to skip this chapter.

If you are willing to give it a shot, get ready to read the next 6 verses out loud 50 times which will take you about an hour.

If you don't have an hour, run through them 25 times which will only take you about 30 minutes.

Or commit to whatever you can.

Anything and everything you do here will help moving forward.

Please note, I left the verse numbers in the passage for your reference only.

When you are ready, begin.

31 For you can all prophesy one by one, so that all may learn and all be encouraged, 32 and the spirits of prophets are subject to prophets. 33 For God is not a God of confusion but of peace. As in all the churches of the saints, 34 the women should keep silent in the churches. For they are not permitted to speak, but should be in submission, as the Law also says. 35 If there is anything they desire to learn, let them ask their husbands at home. For it is shameful for a woman to speak in church. 36 Or was it from you that the word of God came? Or are you the only ones it has reached? (1 Corinthians 14:31-36)

See you tomorrow!

1 Corinthians 14:31

Today you are going to memorize 1 Corinthians 14:31.

After you review what you have already learned, you are going to memorize today's verse using the 10-10-10 Method.

Let's begin.

Let's review the verse you learned yesterday by reciting it 10 times from memory. Glance over it if you need a refresher.

"If a revelation is made to another sitting there, let the first be silent" (1 Corinthians 14:30).

Now you're going to review all the verses you have memorized up to this point by reciting them 10 times. You can find it in the prep work chapter for this week if you need a refresher. If after three times you feel confident in your ability to recite all the verses you have currently memorized, feel free to call it good enough.

When your review is done, let's get into today's verse.

Say the following verse out loud 10 times:

"For you can all prophesy one by one, so that all may learn and all be encouraged" (1 Corinthians 14:31).

When you are done, recite the verse 10 times in a row from memory, doing your best not to look at the verse.

Great job! You got your next verse down!

You know the drill, throughout your day when you're driving to work, taking a break from work, or cooking a meal, go over what you've memorized so far to keep reinforcing it in your mind.

Tomorrow you'll quickly review what you learned today and add another verse to it.

If you don't feel confident you've truly memorized today's verse, consider listening through the chapter again.

See you tomorrow!

God bless.

1 Corinthians 14:32

Today you are going to memorize 1 Corinthians 14:32.

After you review what you have already learned, you are going to memorize today's verse using the 10-10-10 Method.

Let's begin.

Let's review the verse you learned yesterday by reciting it 10 times from memory. Glance over it if you need a refresher.

"For you can all prophesy one by one, so that all may learn and all be encouraged" (1 Corinthians 14:31).

Now you're going to review all the verses you have memorized up to this point by reciting them 10 times. You can find it in the prep work chapter for this week if you need a refresher. If after three times you feel confident in your ability to recite all the verses you have currently memorized, feel free to call it good enough.

When your review is done, let's get into today's verse.

Say the following verse out loud 10 times:

"And the spirits of prophets are subject to prophets" (1 Corinthians 14:32).

When you are done, recite the verse 10 times in a row from memory, doing your best not to look at the verse.

Great job! You got your next verse down!

You know the drill, throughout your day when you're driving to work, taking a break from work, or cooking a meal, go over what you've memorized so far to keep reinforcing it in your mind.

Tomorrow you'll quickly review what you learned today and add another verse to it.

If you don't feel confident you've truly memorized today's verse, consider listening through the chapter again.

See you tomorrow!

God bless.

1 Corinthians 14:33

Today you are going to memorize 1 Corinthians 14:33.

After you review what you have already learned, you are going to memorize today's verse using the 10-10-10 Method.

Let's begin.

Let's review the verse you learned yesterday by reciting it 10 times from memory. Glance over it if you need a refresher.

"And the spirits of prophets are subject to prophets" (1 Corinthians 14:32).

Now you're going to review all the verses you have memorized up to this point by reciting them 10 times. You can find it in the prep work chapter for this week if you need a refresher. If after three times you feel confident in your ability to recite all the verses you have currently memorized, feel free to call it good enough.

When your review is done, let's get into today's verse.

Say the following verse out loud 10 times:

"For God is not a God of confusion but of peace. As in all the churches of the

saints" (1 Corinthians 14:33).

When you are done, recite the verse 10 times in a row from memory, doing your best not to look at the verse.

Great job! You got your next verse down!

You know the drill, throughout your day when you're driving to work, taking a break from work, or cooking a meal, go over what you've memorized so far to keep reinforcing it in your mind.

Tomorrow you'll quickly review what you learned today and add another verse to it.

If you don't feel confident you've truly memorized today's verse, consider listening through the chapter again.

See you tomorrow!

God bless!

1 Corinthians 14:34

Today you are going to memorize 1 Corinthians 14:34.

After you review what you have already learned, you are going to memorize today's verse using the 10-10-10 Method.

Let's begin.

Let's review the verse you learned yesterday by reciting it 10 times from memory. Glance over it if you need a refresher.

"For God is not a God of confusion but of peace. As in all the churches of the saints" (1 Corinthians 14:33).

Now you're going to review all the verses you have memorized up to this point by reciting them 10 times. You can find it in the prep work chapter for this week if you need a refresher. If after three times you feel confident in your ability to recite all the verses you have currently memorized, feel free to call it good enough.

When your review is done, let's get into today's verse.

Say the following verse out loud 10 times:

"The women should keep silent in the churches. For they are not permitted to speak, but should be in submission, as the Law also says" (1 Corinthians 14:34).

When you are done, recite the verse 10 times in a row from memory, doing your best not to look at the verse.

Great job! You got your next verse down!

You know the drill, throughout your day when you're driving to work, taking a break from work, or cooking a meal, go over what you've memorized so far to keep reinforcing it in your mind.

Tomorrow you'll quickly review what you learned today and add another verse to it.

If you don't feel confident you've truly memorized today's verse, consider listening through the chapter again.

See you tomorrow!

God bless!

1 Corinthians 14:35

Today you are going to memorize 1 Corinthians 14:35.

After you review what you have already learned, you are going to memorize today's verse using the 10-10-10 Method.

Let's begin.

Let's review the verse you learned yesterday by reciting it 10 times from memory. Glance over it if you need a refresher.

"The women should keep silent in the churches. For they are not permitted to speak, but should be in submission, as the Law also says" (1 Corinthians 14:34).

Now you're going to review all the verses you have memorized up to this point by reciting them 10 times. You can find it in the prep work chapter for this week if you need a refresher. If after three times you feel confident in your ability to recite all the verses you have currently memorized, feel free to call it good enough.

When your review is done, let's get into today's verse.

Say the following verse out loud 10 times:

"If there is anything they desire to learn, let them ask their husbands at home. For it is shameful for a woman to speak in church" (1 Corinthians 14:35).

When you are done, recite the verse 10 times in a row from memory, doing your best not to look at the verse.

Great job! You got your next verse down!

You know the drill, throughout your day when you're driving to work, taking a break from work, or cooking a meal, go over what you've memorized so far to keep reinforcing it in your mind.

Tomorrow you'll quickly review what you learned today and add another verse to it.

If you don't feel confident you've truly memorized today's verse, consider listening through the chapter again.

See you tomorrow!

God bless!

1 Corinthians 14:36

Today you are going to memorize 1 Corinthians 14:36.

After you review what you have already learned, you are going to memorize today's verse using the 10-10-10 Method.

Let's begin.

Let's review the verse you learned yesterday by reciting it 10 times from memory. Glance over it if you need a refresher.

"If there is anything they desire to learn, let them ask their husbands at home. For it is shameful for a woman to speak in church" (1 Corinthians 14:35).

Now you're going to review all the verses you have memorized up to this point by reciting them 10 times. You can find it in the prep work chapter for this week if you need a refresher. If after three times you feel confident in your ability to recite all the verses you have currently memorized, feel free to call it good enough.

When your review is done, let's get into today's verse.

Say the following verse out loud 10 times:

"Or was it from you that the word of God came? Or are you the only ones it has reached?" (1 Corinthians 14:36).

When you are done, recite the verse 10 times in a row from memory, doing your best not to look at the verse.

Great job! You got your next verse down!

You know the drill, throughout your day when you're driving to work, taking a break from work, or cooking a meal, go over what you've memorized so far to keep reinforcing it in your mind.

Tomorrow you have the optional prep work for the last block of 4 verses. Though it's not mandatory, I can't stress enough how beneficial it will be moving forward.

If you plan to skip it, simply move to the following chapter to begin memorizing the first verse of the last block of 4 verses.

If you don't feel confident you've truly memorized today's verse, consider listening through the chapter again.

See you tomorrow!

God bless.

Week 7 Prep Work

If you are here, that tells me you are ready for your last block of verses to memorize.

Great job so far. I know it takes a lot of time and effort to memorize scripture and I hope all that time and effort has been a joyful experience.

Just like with the first round of prep work, this is completely optional.

You are not required to do this to memorize the last block of 4 verses.

But like I said before, it will make the task much easier.

If you are not up for the prep work, feel free to skip this chapter.

If you are willing to give it a shot, get ready to read the last 4 verses out loud 50 times which will take you about 40 minutes.

If you don't have 40 minutes, run through them 25 times which will only take you about 20 minutes.

Or commit to whatever you can.

Anything and everything you do here will help moving forward.

Please note, I left the verse numbers in the passage for your reference only.

When you are ready, begin.

37 If anyone thinks that he is a prophet, or spiritual, he should acknowledge that the things I am writing to you are a command of the Lord. 38 If anyone does not recognize this, he is not recognized. 39 So, my brothers, earnestly desire to prophesy, and do not forbid speaking in tongues. 40 But all things should be done decently and in order. (1 Corinthians 14:37-40)

See you tomorrow!

1 Corinthians 14:37

Today you are going to memorize 1 Corinthians 14:37.

After you review what you have already learned, you are going to memorize today's verse using the 10-10-10 Method.

Let's begin.

Let's review the verse you learned yesterday by reciting it 10 times from memory. Glance over it if you need a refresher.

"Or was it from you that the word of God came? Or are you the only ones it has reached?" (1 Corinthians 14:36).

Now you're going to review all the verses you have memorized up to this point by reciting them 10 times. You can find it in the prep work chapter for this week if you need a refresher. If after three times you feel confident in your ability to recite all the verses you have currently memorized, feel free to call it good enough.

When your review is done, let's get into today's verse.

Say the following verse out loud 10 times:

"If anyone thinks that he is a prophet, or spiritual, he should acknowledge that the things I am writing to you are a command of the Lord" (1 Corinthians 14:37).

When you are done, recite the verse 10 times in a row from memory, doing your best not to look at the verse.

Great job! You got your next verse down!

You know the drill, throughout your day when you're driving to work, taking a break from work, or cooking a meal, go over what you've memorized so far to keep reinforcing it in your mind.

Tomorrow you'll quickly review what you learned today and add another verse to it.

If you don't feel confident you've truly memorized today's verse, consider listening through the chapter again.

See you tomorrow!

God bless.

1 Corinthians 14:38

Today you are going to memorize 1 Corinthians 14:38.

After you review what you have already learned, you are going to memorize today's verse using the 10-10-10 Method.

Let's begin.

Let's review the verse you learned yesterday by reciting it 10 times from memory. Glance over it if you need a refresher.

"If anyone thinks that he is a prophet, or spiritual, he should acknowledge that the things I am writing to you are a command of the Lord" (1 Corinthians 14:37).

Now you're going to review all the verses you have memorized up to this point by reciting them 10 times. You can find it in the prep work chapter for this week if you need a refresher. If after three times you feel confident in your ability to recite all the verses you have currently memorized, feel free to call it good enough.

When your review is done, let's get into today's verse.

Say the following verse out loud 10 times:

"If anyone does not recognize this, he is not recognized" (1 Corinthians 14:38).

When you are done, recite the verse 10 times in a row from memory, doing your best not to look at the verse.

Great job! You got your next verse down!

You know the drill, throughout your day when you're driving to work, taking a break from work, or cooking a meal, go over what you've memorized so far to keep reinforcing it in your mind.

Tomorrow you'll quickly review what you learned today and add another verse to it.

If you don't feel confident you've truly memorized today's verse, consider listening through the chapter again.

See you tomorrow!

God bless.

1 Corinthians 14:39

Today you are going to memorize 1 Corinthians 14:39.

After you review what you have already learned, you are going to memorize today's verse using the 10-10-10 Method.

Let's begin.

Let's review the verse you learned yesterday by reciting it 10 times from memory. Glance over it if you need a refresher.

"If anyone does not recognize this, he is not recognized" (1 Corinthians 14:38).

Now you're going to review all the verses you have memorized up to this point by reciting them 10 times. You can find it in the prep work chapter for this week if you need a refresher. If after three times you feel confident in your ability to recite all the verses you have currently memorized, feel free to call it good enough.

When your review is done, let's get into today's verse.

Say the following verse out loud 10 times:

"So, my brothers, earnestly desire to prophesy, and do not forbid speaking in tongues" (1 Corinthians 14:39).

When you are done, recite the verse 10 times in a row from memory, doing your best not to look at the verse.

Great job! You got your next verse down!

You know the drill, throughout your day when you're driving to work, taking a break from work, or cooking a meal, go over what you've memorized so far to keep reinforcing it in your mind.

Tomorrow you'll quickly review what you learned today and add another verse to it.

If you don't feel confident you've truly memorized today's verse, consider listening through the chapter again.

See you tomorrow!

God bless!

1 Corinthians 14:40

Today you are going to memorize 1 Corinthians 14:40.

After you review what you have already learned, you are going to memorize today's verse using the 10-10-10 Method.

Let's begin.

Let's review the verse you learned yesterday by reciting it 10 times from memory. Glance over it if you need a refresher.

"So, my brothers, earnestly desire to prophesy, and do not forbid speaking in tongues" (1 Corinthians 14:39).

Now you're going to review all the verses you have memorized up to this point by reciting them 10 times. You can find it in the prep work chapter for this week if you need a refresher. If after three times you feel confident in your ability to recite all the verses you have currently memorized, feel free to call it good enough.

When your review is done, let's get into today's verse.

Say the following verse out loud 10 times:

"But all things should be done decently and in order" **(1 Corinthians 14:40).**

When you are done, recite the verse 10 times in a row from memory, doing your best not to look at the verse.

Great job! You got your last verse down!

You know the drill, throughout your day when you're driving to work, taking a break from work, or cooking a meal, go over what you've memorized so far to keep reinforcing it in your mind.

If you don't feel confident you've truly memorized today's verse, consider listening through the chapter again.

God bless!

Conclusion

If you are here, I hope that means you have fully memorized 1 Corinthians 14.

I hope the experience was rewarding and enriching as you sealed part of God's Word in your heart.

I recommend reciting the full passage every day for the next 30 days to truly solidify that piece of scripture in your mind.

Once you're done, consider memorizing another passage or even an entire book of the Bible!

Lastly, if you have enjoyed this book, do consider leaving a review. I look forward to seeing your feedback.

May God bless you on your journey to further know Him, and I leave you with these two verses, "All Scripture is breathed out by God and profitable for teaching, for reproof, for correction, and for training in righteousness, that the man of God may be complete, equipped for every good work" (2 Timothy 3:16-17).

www.ingramcontent.com/pod-product-compliance
Lightning Source LLC
Chambersburg PA
CBHW022010120526
44592CB00034B/767